THE HUBBLE SPACE TELESCOPE

OUR EYE ON THE UNIVERSE

Terence Dickinson with Tracy C. Read

THE HUBBLE
SPACE TELESCOPE

OUR EYE ON THE UNIVERSE

FIREFLY BOOKS

A FIREFLY BOOK

Published by Firefly Books Ltd. 2019

First printing

Library of Congress Control Number: 2019935970

Library and Archives Canada Cataloguing in Publication
Title: The Hubble Space Telescope : our eye on the universe /
 Terence Dickinson with Tracy C. Read.

Names: Dickinson, Terence, author. | Read, Tracy C., author.

Description: Includes index.

Identifiers: Canadiana 20190080620 |
 ISBN 9780228102335 (hardcover) |
 ISBN 9780228102175 (softcover)

Subjects: LCSH: Hubble Space Telescope (Spacecraft)—Juvenile
 literature. | LCSH: Astronomy—Research—Juvenile literature. |
 LCSH: Space telescopes—Juvenile literature. | LCSH: Space
 photography—Juvenile literature.

Classification: LCC QB500.268 .D53 2019 | DDC j522/.2919—dc23

For Susan and Janice,
our stellar companions

Published in the United States by
Firefly Books (U.S.) Inc.
P.O. Box 1338, Ellicott Station
Buffalo, New York 14205

Published in Canada by
Firefly Books Ltd.
50 Staples Avenue, Unit 1
Richmond Hill, Ontario L4B 0A7

Cover and interior design:
Janice McLean/Bookmakers Press Inc.

Printed in China

Canada

*We acknowledge the financial support
of the Government of Canada.*

Front cover: Crab Nebula/NASA, ESA, G. Dubner (IAFE, CONICET-University of Buenos Aires) et al.; A. Loll et al.; T. Temim et al.; F. Seward et al.; VLA/NRAO/AUI/NSF; Chandra/CXC; Spitzer/JPL-Caltech; XMM-Newton/ESA; and Hubble/STScI
Front cover, inset: NASA
Back cover: ARP 273, a pair of interacting galaxies in the constellation Andromeda/NASA, ESA, Hubble Heritage Team (STScI/AURA)
Back cover, inset: NASA

CONTENTS

CENTER OF THE MILKY WAY

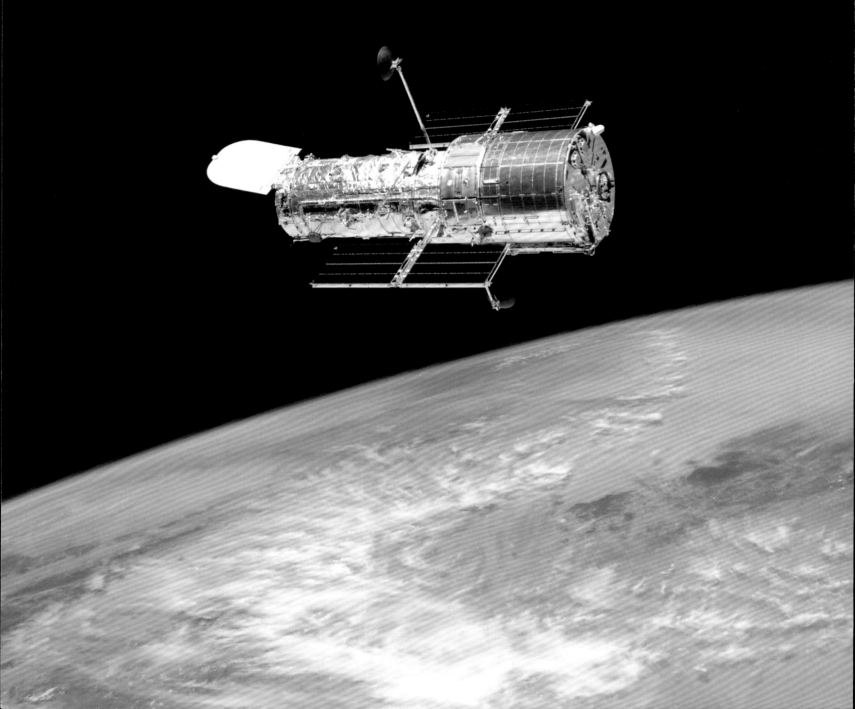

HIGH FLIGHT After its launch into space aboard the space shuttle Discovery on April 24, 1990, the Hubble Space Telescope was placed in orbit some 340 miles (550 km) above the Earth's surface. There, in the pristine darkness of space, it began one of the most successful and exciting science missions in history. Right: In the first of five space-walks to fine-tune, update and repair Hubble's scientific payload for the final time, astronaut John Grunsfeld works on the orbiting observatory on May 14, 2009.

OUR EYE ON THE UNIVERSE

ASTRO MECHANIC

Until Galileo first pointed his small telescope at the night sky in 1609 and went on to discover moons orbiting Jupiter, stars in the Milky Way and Venus going through phases like the Moon, everything we knew about our universe came from simple observations with the unaided eye. The Italian astronomer had set in motion a celestial revolution.

The next centuries brought larger and more powerful telescopes. Observatories were built in dark rural locations or on remote mountaintops to avoid the light that spills into the night sky in densely populated areas and washes out faint celestial objects. Still, the ground-based instruments had to look through the Earth's atmosphere, a churning blanket of gas and dust. But with the launch of the Hubble Space Telescope in 1990, astronomers had a major telescope positioned in space, well beyond the Earth's distorting atmosphere.

Hubble has an impressive track record. It has traveled three billion miles (5 billion km), circling Earth nearly 150,000 times. It has taken over half a million images. The data it has collected would fill 50 million books. Its reach has extended from the solar system to the edge of the known universe. It has had a major impact in every area of astronomy. And, after nearly three decades, Hubble soldiers on.

Like a time machine, Hubble has transported us back to the early years of our 13.8-billion-year-old universe and unveiled a rough-and-tumble realm of violent explosions, cataclysmic collisions and firestorms of gas and dust forging new stars. Along the way, it has captured stunning portraits of deep space and introduced us to a universe that is awesome, chaotic and mysterious.

Hubble boldly ushered us into a new golden age of astronomy.

↑ SAY CHEESE While perched on the space shuttle's robotic arm, astronaut Andrew Feustel took this photo of John Grunsfeld during the final servicing mission to Hubble in 2009. His reflection can be seen in Grunsfeld's visor.

← EARLY CRISIS Hubble's road to success has been bumpy. Just weeks after its launch, Hubble was sending back blurry images. A monumental blunder had occurred. The telescope's main mirror had been ground to the wrong prescription. It was like putting on a friend's glasses and experiencing blurred vision. Computers were able to remove much of the blur, but at a cost: A lot of light had to be taken from the images, preventing Hubble from seeing very faint objects. Three years later, in 1993, astronauts aboard the space shuttle Endeavour paid Hubble a visit and installed corrective optics to fix the problem.

⬇ BY THE NUMBERS During a servicing mission to Hubble in 1997, an astronaut removes a spectrograph (an instrument that breaks light into a spectrum) before installing new equipment. The Hubble Telescope is the length of a large school bus (43½ feet/13. 2 m) and weighs 27,000 pounds (10,900 kg), about the same as two adult African elephants. Its primary mirror—Hubble's eye in the sky—measures 94.5 inches (2.4 m) across. Two winglike solar arrays collect energy from the Sun and convert it to electricity to power Hubble. One orbit around Earth takes about 97 minutes.

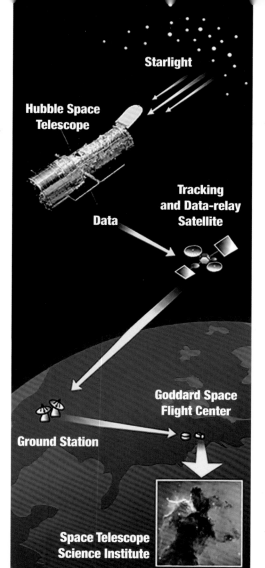

Starlight

Hubble Space Telescope

Data

Tracking and Data-relay Satellite

Ground Station

Goddard Space Flight Center

Space Telescope Science Institute

← RELAY TEAM Like the Olympic torch bearers who carry the flame across country and into the stadium, it takes a dedicated team of engineers and computer scientists to bring home the information Hubble gathers. All the directions and commands that tell Hubble what to do come from the Flight Operations Team at the Goddard Space Flight Center, in Greenbelt, Maryland. Hubble has two main computers on board and several smaller systems. One of the primary computers points the telescope; the other runs the scientific instruments, receiving and sending the data they gather to satellites that relay it to a ground station in White Sands, New Mexico. The data is then transmitted from the ground station to Goddard. From there, it is sent to the Space Telescope Science Institute, in Baltimore, Maryland. There, the data are translated and stored. Hubble sends enough information to fill about 18 DVDs every week. Astronomers can access and download the Hubble data via the Internet from anywhere in the world.

WHO WAS EDWIN HUBBLE? Like his namesake, Edwin Hubble (1889-1953) revolutionized our understanding of the universe and our place in it. As a young man, Hubble excelled at sports, but he went on to study mathematics, law and astronomy. After earning a PhD in astronomy, he went to work at the Mount Wilson Observatory, in California. Most astronomers of the day thought that the entire universe—everything we could see with the unaided eye and with the most powerful telescopes—was contained within the Milky Way Galaxy. Hubble spent long, weary hours at the eyepiece of the 100-inch Hooker telescope, then the largest telescope in the world, and studied photographs taken by the instrument. He discovered that there were other galaxies beyond the Milky Way and that they are speeding away from one another. This gave rise to the Big Bang theory, which speculates that the universe began at a single point with a colossal explosion of energy and matter.

PART 1 ALL ABOUT HUBBLE

Primary Mirror Collects light from the telescope's targets and reflects it to a secondary mirror. It is made of a special polished glass coated in aluminum and a compound that reflects ultraviolet light.

Secondary Mirror About 12% of the size of the primary mirror, it reflects light back through a hole in the primary mirror and then to the science instruments.

Aperture Door This door can be closed to prevent direct sunlight from damaging the telescope.

Fine Guidance Sensors Two sensors point and lock the telescope on a target; a third sensor precisely measures star positions.

Communication Antennas Images and data are converted to radio waves, which are beamed through one of the antennas to a NASA satellite and from there to Earth.

Space Telescope Imaging Spectrograph Acts like a prism by separating light into individual colors, providing a wavelength "fingerprint" of the target object. This tells us about its temperature, chemistry, density and motion.

Cosmic Origins Spectrograph The most sensitive ultraviolet spectrograph in space is helping astronomers better understand the "cosmic web" of gas that stretches between galaxies and the formation and evolution of galaxies, stars and planets.

Solar Panels The "power plant" for operating Hubble, the solar arrays convert sunlight into electricity.

Near Infrared Camera and Multi-Object Spectrometer Detects infrared light, so it can see objects that are otherwise hidden by dust and gas. It is inactive at present.

Advanced Camera for Surveys Installed in 2002, it became Hubble's most heavily used instrument. It took the first image of a planet orbiting another star.

Wide Field Camera 3 Studies a wide range of celestial objects and phenomena. Working with the Advanced Camera for Surveys, it spotted one of the youngest galaxies ever seen (just 420 million years old). It also discovered the fourth and fifth moons circling Pluto.

HUBBLE'S TOP DISCOVERIES

1 Hubble has identified objects that existed only 450 million years after the Big Bang, helping scientists understand how the universe is evolving.

2 Using Hubble, astronomers have determined that every major galaxy has a massive black hole at its center—and the bigger the galaxy's central bulge of stars, the more massive the black hole.

3 We now know a great deal about the atmospheres of Jupiter-like planets that orbit around stars other than our Sun.

4 Hubble can detect objects at greater distances, allowing astronomers to refine the expansion rate of the universe and its age (13.8 billion years).

5 It may be invisible, but dark matter rules! We know it's there because its gravity distorts the light of distant galaxies. Aided by Hubble, astronomers have created a map showing a network of dark matter throughout space.

6 Edwin Hubble discovered the universe is expanding in all directions. The Hubble Telescope determined the universe is expanding faster now than earlier in its history. Dark energy, a mysterious, invisible force, is powering this acceleration.

⬆ CHANDRA X-RAY OBSERVATORY In orbit since 1999, Chandra detects X-ray emissions from very hot sources in the universe, such as clusters of galaxies, exploded stars and matter around black holes.

WITH A LITTLE HELP FROM ITS FRIENDS

The idea behind NASA's Great Observatories was to have four orbiting observatories, each studying regions of space in a different wavelength, to give the most complete picture of objects in the cosmos. It was compared to hearing an entire symphony instead of a solo instrument. Hubble, the program's centerpiece, gathers visible, ultraviolet and near-infrared light. The Compton Gamma Ray Observatory was designed to observe high-energy gamma rays. Launched in 1991, it reentered the Earth's atmosphere in 2000, after it had collected data on some of the most violent events in the universe. Chandra and Spitzer, seen here, continue to play an important role.

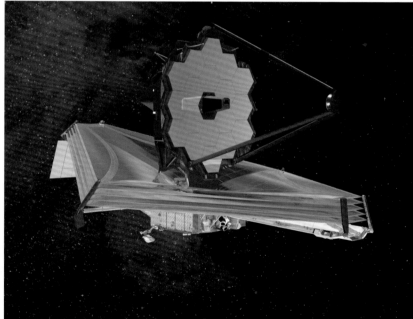

⬆ SPITZER SPACE TELESCOPE This orbiting telescope has been following the Earth's path around the Sun since 2003. Its infrared view of the universe allows us to see regions of space that are hidden from optical telescopes, including dusty stellar nurseries, the centers of galaxies and newly forming planetary systems.

⬆ JAMES WEBB SPACE TELESCOPE With seven times the light-collecting power of Hubble, Webb will peer even deeper into space and further back in time. The telescope will have infrared vision, which Hubble lacks, allowing it to capture the ancient light of stars that formed 200 million years after the Big Bang. It will also search for planets capable of supporting life around stars that are relatively close to our Sun and study the evolution of our solar system. Its launch is currently planned for 2021.

FIELD DAY A bedazzling assortment of galaxies stretches as far as Hubble's eye can see. To capture this image, Hubble focused on a tiny segment of the night sky no bigger than the size of a period in this book held at arm's length. Yet each splash and dot of color is a celestial island of billions of stars adrift in the inky blackness of space.

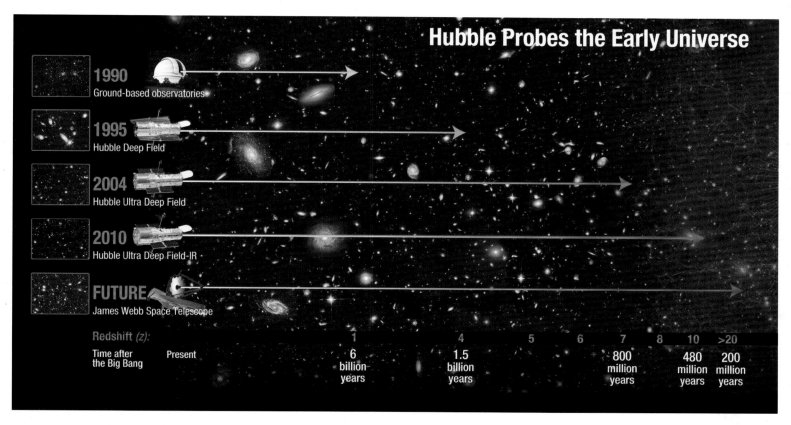

Hubble Probes the Early Universe

1990
Ground-based observatories

1995
Hubble Deep Field

2004
Hubble Ultra Deep Field

2010
Hubble Ultra Deep Field-IR

FUTURE
James Webb Space Telescope

Redshift (z):		1	4	5	6	7	8	10	>20
Time after the Big Bang	Present	6 billion years	1.5 billion years			800 million years		480 million years	200 million years

↑ TIME MACHINE The deeper Hubble peers into space, the further back in time it carries us. When Hubble photographs an object 7,000 light-years away, for example, the light it records has taken 7,000 years to travel through space to reach that camera. So what we see is how the object looked 7,000 years ago. The chart above illustrates how far ground-based telescopes could see in 1990, the year Hubble was launched, and the marked improvement in Hubble's performance as it was upgraded over the years. Our next great leap forward will be with the James Webb Space Telescope.

← FAR OUT Hubble and the Spitzer Space Telescope teamed up to ferret out a primitive galaxy—SPT0615-JD—that existed when the universe was just 500 million years old. It is the most distant galaxy yet seen.

VISIBLE LIGHT

NEAR-INFRARED LIGHT

↑ TWO WAYS OF LOOKING AT IT

This pair of Hubble images could be two completely unrelated celestial objects, but they are both portraits of the Lagoon Nebula, a colossal stellar nursery 4,000 light-years away. Why do they look so different? The photo on the left was taken in visible light, while the one on the right was taken in near-infrared light.

Light travels through space in waves, like the waves formed when a speedboat races across a still lake. The height of the waves and the distance between the crest of each wave vary depending on the color, just as they would if the boat were larger or smaller. This is called a wavelength. Our eyes are sensitive to a narrow range of wavelengths that covers a spectrum of colors, like those in a rainbow. Wavelengths that fall outside that range are invisible to our eyes. Infrared and near-infrared cameras can see wavelengths beyond the visible spectrum. When looking into deep space, astronomers want to be able to gather

as much information as possible about the celestial objects they observe, and that's why Hubble is equipped with cameras that can take images in visible light and near-infrared light.

In the image at left, a huge young star called Herschel 36 at the center of the nebula is releasing blistering radiation and fierce stellar winds that have blown holes in the cocoon of gas and dust surrounding the star. Now look at the star-filled image on the right, taken in near-infrared wavelengths of light. Most of these stars are far beyond the nebula itself. As can be seen when comparing these two photos, infrared observations can look through murky clouds of dust and gas to uncover what is hidden to our eye in visible light. This view primes us for what we can expect when the James Webb Space Telescope is in orbit and fully operational. Its infrared vision will be able to penetrate the dark wisps of nebula that still hide stars in this Hubble near-infrared image.

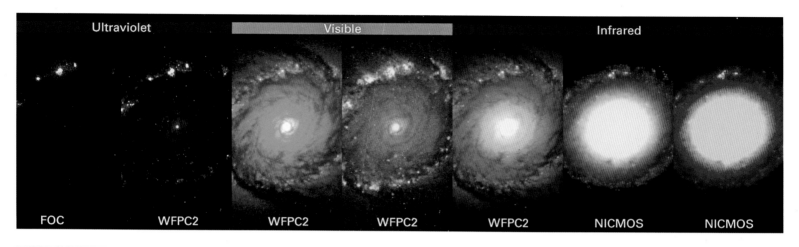

Ultraviolet		Visible		Infrared		
FOC	WFPC2	WFPC2	WFPC2	WFPC2	NICMOS	NICMOS

⬆ RAINBOW BRIGHT Hubble is a great multi-tasker. To produce the spectacular image of a barred spiral galaxy named NGC1512, shown at left, required the use of three cameras and several color filters to tease out details in the photo. At the far left are two ultraviolet images taken by the Faint Object Camera. The next two in line are visible-light images from the Wide Field Planetary Camera 2, and the three images on the right are taken by the Near Infrared Camera and Multi-Object Spectrometer. In the ultraviolet images, clusters of young, hot stars stand out in a ring surrounding the core. By viewing celestial objects in different wavelengths, astronomers can extract more detailed information about their composition and age.

⬅ SPUN GOLD Resembling a jewel-encrusted pot of gold, this image of the center of NGC1512 was created by combining the seven Hubble images shown at the top of this page. The brilliant pink patches encircling the main disk of the galaxy are infant star clusters. NGC1512 lies 30 million light-years away and is a neighbor of our Milky Way Galaxy.

NAVIGATING THE UNIVERSE: A GLOSSARY

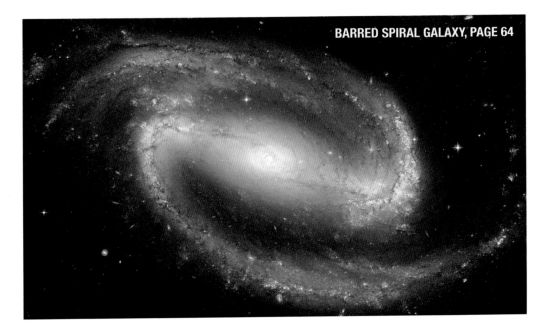

BARRED SPIRAL GALAXY, PAGE 64

asteroid belt A region in the solar system between the four inner planets (Mercury, Venus, Earth, Mars) and the four outer planets (Jupiter, Saturn, Uranus, Neptune) that contains millions of asteroids in orbit around the Sun.

asteroids Rocky bodies floating around in space that are probably leftover material from the formation of the solar system 4.6 billion years ago. They range in size from 600 miles (1,000 km) across (roughly the distance from New York City to Montreal) to mere pebbles.

atmosphere A mixture of gases that envelops a celestial body, such as a planet. It is held in place by that body's gravity. Although the Earth's atmosphere is thin and transparent, it shields us from cosmic rays and other dangerous radiation from the Sun and deep space. It is an insulator too, protecting us from the extreme temperatures of space. Without it, most places on Earth would be either blisteringly hot or frigidly cold, as is the case on the Moon.

aurora Also known as the northern lights and aurora borealis in the northern hemisphere (aurora australis in the southern hemisphere), auroras are caused when electrically charged particles from the Sun encounter the Earth's magnetic field. The particles are funneled along the magnetic lines of force at the north or south magnetic pole, where they interact with the gases in the Earth's upper atmosphere, producing pulsing, wavering bands, curtains or streamers of pinkish or greenish light. Auroras have also been observed on Saturn, Jupiter, Uranus and Neptune.

axis An imaginary line that runs through the center of a planet from the north pole to the south pole. The planet spins around this axis like a spinning top as it orbits the Sun.

barred spiral galaxy In a typical spiral galaxy, the starry arms curve out from the center of the galaxy. In a barred spiral galaxy, a concentration of mostly older stars forms a bar that runs across the middle of the galaxy, and the arms curl outward from the ends of this bar. The Milky Way is a barred spiral galaxy.

Big Bang The explosion that created the universe 13.8 billion years ago. From this extremely dense and hot state, the cosmos has been expanding and evolving ever since.

black hole Some stars end their lives in a colossal explosion, then collapse in on themselves. If the collapsing core of the star is large enough, the matter falling in toward the center crushes itself out of existence. All that remains is an intense gravity field—a black hole. Anything that travels close to the black hole is swallowed up and reduced to the atomic level. Nothing can escape a black hole's deadly pull, not even light, which is why it's black.

comet Often called "dirty snowballs," comets are small bodies of ice and rock a few miles across that are found in the outer realm of the solar system. Occasionally, one plunges in toward the inner solar system. The Sun's heat melts some of the ices in the comet, causing gases to be released into space. These gases form a tail that can be millions of miles long. Some comets disintegrate when they near the Sun; others swing around the Sun and continue in an orbit that brings them back years later.

constellations In ancient times, patterns of stars were given names, and myths and legends were told of the heroes and beasts that made their way across the night sky from season to season. It became a way of mapping the night sky, and we still use these captivating names.

cosmos See *Universe*.

dark energy The mysterious invisible force that scientists believe is responsible for the accelerating expansion of the universe.

dark matter Although we can't see dark matter, astronomers know it's there by the way its gravity distorts the light from distant galaxies. By analyzing Hubble data on those distortions, scientists have mapped out where dark matter is distributed throughout the universe.

dwarf galaxy Compared with the Milky Way Galaxy, which has 200 billion to 400 billion stars, dwarf galaxies contain only a few billion stars and have a fraction of the mass of the Milky Way. The Large Magellanic Cloud is a dwarf galaxy.

dwarf planet In 2006, Pluto lost its status as the ninth planet in our solar system and was designated a dwarf planet by the International Astronomical Union (IAU), which assigns official names and terms for things in space. In order for a body to be called a planet, the IAU said that (1) it must orbit the Sun, (2) it must have enough gravity to pull itself into a round shape and (3) it must have "cleared the

DWARF PLANET, PAGE 29

DWARF GALAXY, PAGE 60

neighborhood" of its orbit, meaning that it has swept away other similar objects in its path around the Sun. Dwarf planets meet the first two standards but flunk the third—they share their region of the solar system with other objects like them.

electromagnetic spectrum All the different kinds of light and energy in the universe, including radio waves, microwaves, infrared radiation, visible light, ultraviolet light, X-rays and gamma rays.

elliptical galaxy Smooth and featureless, elliptical galaxies may be nearly spherical or so elongated they look like a cigar. They are usually found in compact groups of galaxies. Constant mergers and collisions with other galaxies, followed by periods of star formation, increase the size of an elliptical galaxy and use up much of the gas needed to create new stars. As a result, ellipticals contain mostly old red stars and have a very low rate of star formation. With a cargo of hundreds of millions to trillions of stars, ellipticals are the biggest galaxies in the universe.

elongated galaxy Called "tadpoles," elongated galaxies occur in large numbers at greater distances, where we are observing the universe at an earlier time in its history. The Fireworks Galaxy is an example of an elongated galaxy.

extra-solar planet (exoplanet) A planet outside our solar system orbiting another star.

galaxy A stellar city containing vast numbers of stars, nebulas, planets and comets as well as huge quantities of gas and dust, all held together by gravity. Galaxies may be found on their own or in clusters. Astronomers estimate there are at least 100 billion galaxies in the known universe. The galaxy we live in is called the Milky Way.

gamma rays Part of the electromagnetic spectrum, gamma rays have lots of energy. They come from big events like huge eruptions on the Sun called solar flares and exploding stars.

GLOBULAR STAR CLUSTER, PAGE 37

globular star cluster Spherical clusters of up to a million stars bound together by gravity, globular star clusters hold our galaxy's oldest stars. They orbit the core of galaxies like satellites. The Milky Way Galaxy has at least 150 globular clusters. Galaxies larger than the Milky Way can have thousands.

NAVIGATING THE UNIVERSE: A GLOSSARY

gravity The "glue" that holds our solar system, galaxies and clusters of galaxies together. Gravity is a natural force by which a planet or other body draws objects toward its center. The force of gravity keeps the planets in orbit around the Sun.

infrared light Part of the electromagnetic spectrum that we cannot see with our eyes but can feel as heat. It is made of waves released by hot objects, such as stars. Its wavelengths are just a little longer than the wavelengths of red light we can see. Near-infrared light is only a portion of the infrared wavelengths.

irregular galaxy A loose collection of stars with no distinct structure or core, irregular galaxies appear misshapen because they are often within the gravitational influence of nearby galaxies.

Kuiper belt A doughnut-shaped ring of icy objects beyond the orbit of Neptune. Pluto resides in the Kuiper belt.

Large Magellanic Cloud A dwarf galaxy, the Large Magellanic Cloud is a satellite galaxy of the Milky Way and is the nearest galaxy to us.

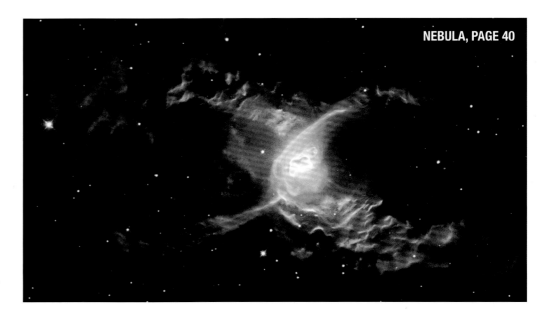

NEBULA, PAGE 40

LARGE MAGELLANIC CLOUD, PAGE 56

light-year The distance light travels in space in a year (six trillion miles/10 trillion km). It is used to measure distances to stars and galaxies from Earth.

mass The amount of matter an object contains.

matter The stuff that everything is made of. Atoms are a tiny bit of matter. Big planets have lots of matter. Even you are made of matter.

Messier catalog A list compiled by French astronomer Charles Messier, published in 1781, that identifies 110 celestial objects in the night sky.

Milky Way Galaxy When we look up on a clear, dark night, we see a hazy band of stars stretching overhead. This is the Milky Way, a barred spiral galaxy. We reside in one of the arms of this spiral galaxy. From the northern hemisphere, the Milky Way is at its brightest in summer, because we are looking toward the central region of our galaxy. In winter, when Earth is at the opposite side of its orbit, we are looking toward the outer part of the galaxy, and the Milky Way is not nearly as bright.

NASA The National Aeronautics and Space Administration is an independent agency of the United States federal government that is responsible for the civilian space program as well as aerospace research. Hubble is one of many NASA projects.

nebula Clouds of gas and dust within a galaxy, nebulas are usually dark, but some are illuminated by nearby stars or stars embedded in them. Some nebulas mark the death of a star; others are stellar nurseries where new stars are forming.

neutron star The size of a mountain, a neutron star has two or three times as much material packed into it as there is in our entire Sun. A teaspoonful of neutron-star material would weigh more than a million railroad locomotives. It has a very powerful gravitational force.

NGC Using the prefix "NGC" followed by a number, the New General Catalogue of Nebulae and Clusters of Stars identifies thousands of deep-sky objects, galaxies, star clusters and nebulas.

open star cluster A group of young stars briefly held together by gravity, an open star cluster is born inside dense clouds of matter in our galaxy. Most open clusters have a short life (by astronomical standards), usually breaking apart in less than 100 million years.

orbit The curved path that a planet, satellite or spacecraft follows as it moves around another object.

planet A large body in outer space that orbits around the Sun or another star.

red giant star As a star ages and cools, its outer shell expands and burns in a reddish color as its center collapses, becoming a red giant.

solar system Eight planets and their dozens of moons, millions of asteroids and trillions of comets are all members of the solar system. The Sun is at the center, and its gravity rules the orbital paths of everything else.

spiral galaxy Long stellar arms wind around a large central bulge, like a slowly rotating celestial pinwheel. New stars form mostly in the spiral arms, while the center contains older, dimmer stars.

star Stars are enormous spheres of burning, erupting gases that emit vast quantities of heat and energy into space. Our Sun is a medium-

SPIRAL GALAXY, PAGE 55

sized star. Stars are born in vast clouds of gas and dust called nebulas. They are the building blocks of every galaxy.

stellar wind A constant stream of particles and energy emitted by the Sun.

Sun The star in the center of our solar system.

supernova When a massive star runs out of hydrogen fuel, it expands to become a red giant. The core eventually collapses, and the outer layers start to cave in, only to be hurled out again by a raging torrent of subatomic particles. The exploding gases glare billions of times brighter than an ordinary star in a supernova explosion that often outshines its own galaxy.

universe All of space and time, and everything in it. It's everything ever!

visible light The part of the electromagnetic spectrum that we can see with our eyes. It's all the colors of the rainbow.

white dwarf star A star about the size of Earth but with the mass of the Sun. Its matter is very densely packed. A teaspoonful of white-dwarf material would weigh as much as a car. Sirius B is a white dwarf star.

MARS

URANUS

JUPITER

SATURN

PLUTO

OUR SOLAR SYSTEM

The eight planets in our solar system travel in elliptical (oval-shaped) orbits around the biggest object found here—the huge, hot star we know as the Sun. The four inner planets closest to the Sun—Mercury, Venus, Earth and Mars—are small, rocky worlds. Because of their solid surfaces, they are known as "terrestrial" planets. They contain various heavy metals like iron and nickel. The inner planets have few or no moons. Earth, as we know, has one moon, while Mars has two tiny moons. Mercury and Venus have none.

An asteroid belt containing millions of small, rocky bodies separates the four inner planets from the four much larger outer planets—Jupiter, Saturn, Uranus and Neptune. Asteroids range in size from 600 miles (1,000 km) across to mere pebbles. These bits of debris are left over from the solar system's formation approximately 4.6 billion years ago.

The four outer planets are giants compared to the terrestrial planets. Each of these colossal worlds has a rocky core surrounded by an atmosphere of compressed gases thousands of miles deep. And each has a family of a dozen or more moons. Jupiter has at least 80!

One of Hubble's many contributions has been its decades-long observation of the dramatic weather systems visible in the planets' atmospheres. It has documented high winds, violent storms and other extreme activity that flyby satellites are unable to record.

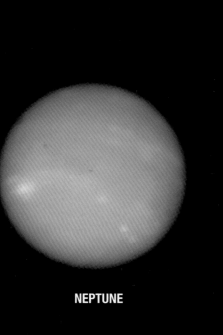

NEPTUNE

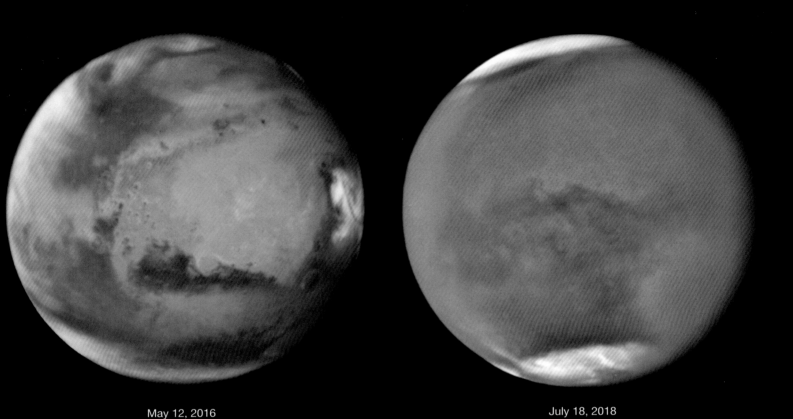

May 12, 2016

July 18, 2018

LIFE ON THE RED PLANET?

In the late 1800s, telescopes became powerful enough to reveal features on Mars that reminded astronomers of Earth. They observed deserts and dark regions that changed with the Martian seasons and polar caps that expanded in the Martian winter and grew smaller in summer. From time to time, clouds and dust storms appeared. These observations inspired almost a century of lively discussions about whether higher forms of life might live on the red planet. But in the 1960s and 1970s, when the first few spacecraft to reach Mars revealed a landscape that resembles the Moon much more than Earth, the idea of life on Mars was finally put to rest.

CLEAR SKIES AND DUST DEVILS Imagine an invisible line running through Earth from the North Pole to the South Pole (you can picture the same thing with the top and bottom of an orange). All planets spin around this "axis" as they orbit the Sun. For the half of the planet that is tilted toward the Sun, it is summer. For the half that tilts away, it is winter. Earth and Mars are both tilted at a similar angle, but Mars takes roughly twice as long as Earth to complete a single orbit around the Sun: 687 days compared with the Earth's 365 days. The seasons on Mars are also twice as long as they are on Earth, and they are more extreme. We see very different versions of Mars above. In the 2016 image, it's a clear day and the northern hemisphere is tilted toward Earth. In the 2018 image, the heat from the southern hemisphere's spring and summer has kicked up a global dust storm in the lowest point on the planet—you can see the swirling clouds over the South Pole.

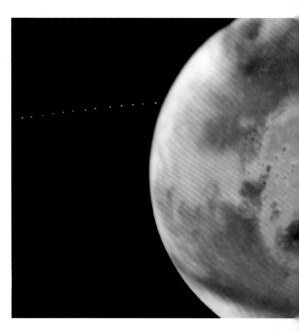

➡ **A MINIATURE MOON IN MOTION** Phobos, one of the two moons of Mars, can be seen tracking across the Martian sky in this image, which combines 13 Hubble exposures. Football-shaped Phobos measures only 14 miles (22.7 km) across and looks more like a star here than a moon. It orbits a mere 5,827 miles (9,377 km) above Mars—our Moon orbits 238,863 miles (384,412 km) above Earth. The tiny moon completes three orbits in one Martian day, which is a little longer than our 24-hour day.

⬇ **MARS UNRAVELED** Created from individual Hubble images of Mars, this photo map spans most of the planet's surface. Mars is covered with fine, dry orange dust made of iron oxide, or rust. Coarser dust looks darker. Observing through his telescope in the late 19th century, astronomer Percival Lowell thought he was seeing canals crossing the Martian deserts. The harder he looked, the more canals he saw—or *thought* he saw. Lowell speculated that the canals were built by a Martian civilization. But by the 1960s, close-up spacecraft images of the red planet revealed the real Mars: a complex desert world of sand dunes, volcanoes, craters and canyons—but no canals.

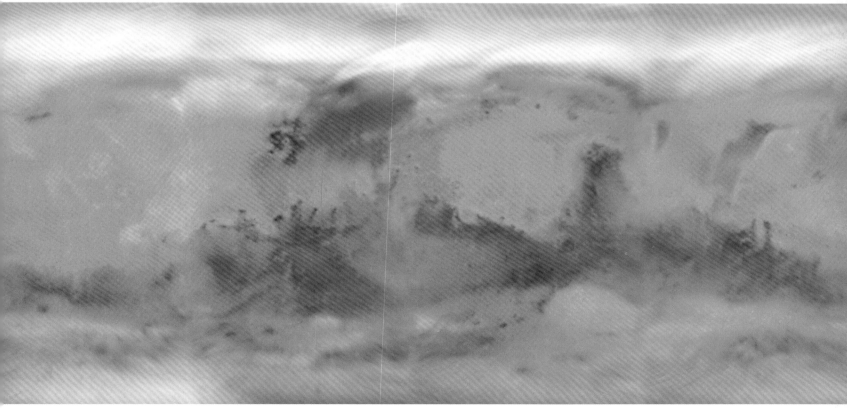

JUST DROPPING BY Jupiter is roughly 2½ times the mass of all the other planets in the solar system combined, and it has the moon power to go with its bulk: at least 80 known moons. This image was taken by the Hubble Space Telescope on April 9, 2007. It captures Jupiter's largest moon, Ganymede, just before it slipped out of view behind the colossal planet. Ganymede is about one-third the diameter of Earth. In 2015, Hubble observations of the supersized moon offered evidence that Ganymede may have an underground saltwater ocean containing more water than exists on the Earth's surface. Jupiter has three more large moons and dozens of smaller ones.

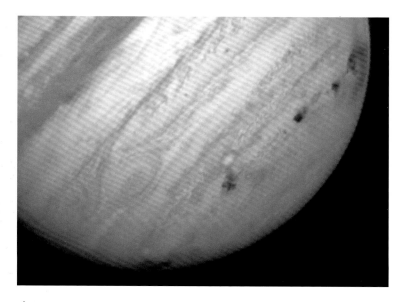

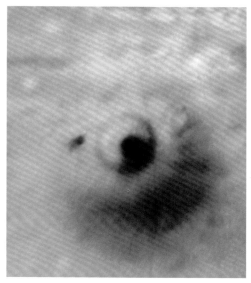

JUPITER
The largest of the solar system's giant planets, Jupiter is a huge world made mostly of gases. No solid ground exists on Jupiter or any of the giant outer planets. Jupiter's famous Great Red Spot is a fierce storm in the big planet's atmosphere that is almost twice the Earth's diameter. It has been observed by astronomers for more than 150 years.

⬆ **BRUISED BUT NOT BROKEN** From July 16 to 22, 1994, 20 fragments from Comet Shoemaker-Levy 9 exploded upon impact with Jupiter, leaving dark bruises on the giant planet—shown in both images above—that astronomy hobbyists were able to see through their backyard telescopes for weeks. This once-in-a-lifetime mash-up was recorded by the Hubble Space Telescope. In the lower cloud band, above left, note the oval-shaped Great Red Spot, which in recent years Hubble has revealed is more orange than red and more round than oval.

⬇ **THE WHOLE ROLL** Imagine peeling Jupiter's atmospheric "skin" like an orange and then flattening it. The image below was made by digitally flattening several Hubble photos to show the entire planet.

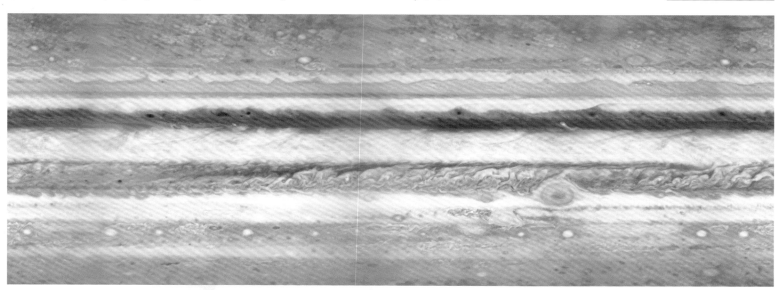

➜ RING THEORY Saturn's famous rings contain trillions of icy particles that may have resulted from a collision of large moons billions of years ago. The rings are about as wide as the distance from Earth to the Moon but as little as 330 feet (100 m) thick. The particles range in size from bits too tiny to see to some that are bigger than a school bus. When Galileo first spotted Saturn's rings through his telescope in 1610, he thought they might be large moons positioned on either side of the planet.

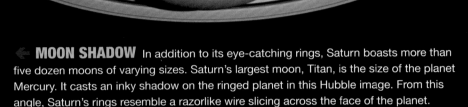

← MOON SHADOW In addition to its eye-catching rings, Saturn boasts more than five dozen moons of varying sizes. Saturn's largest moon, Titan, is the size of the planet Mercury. It casts an inky shadow on the ringed planet in this Hubble image. From this angle, Saturn's rings resemble a razorlike wire slicing across the face of the planet.

⬇ MAXIMUM TILT Saturn is close to its maximum tilt toward Earth in this Hubble photograph taken on June 6, 2018, presenting an incredible view of its rings and the gaps between them. The largest gap, known as the Cassini Division, separates the outer rings A and B. The bright clouds visible along the lower edge of Saturn's North Pole are leftovers from a massive storm.

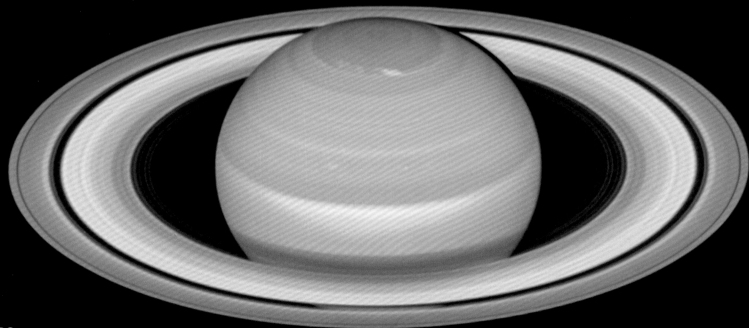

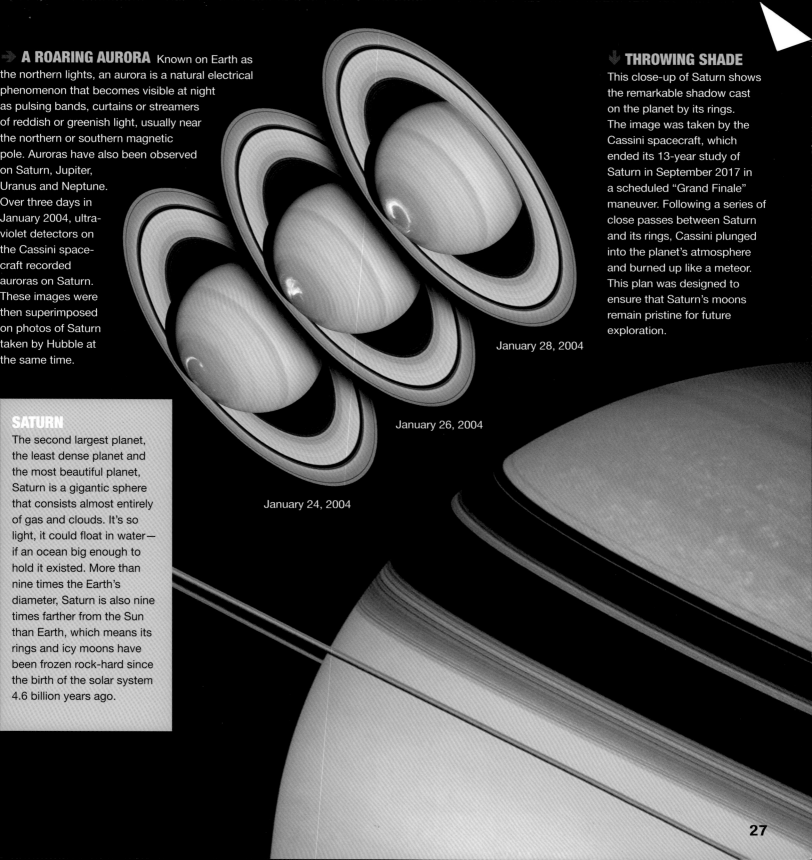

A ROARING AURORA Known on Earth as the northern lights, an aurora is a natural electrical phenomenon that becomes visible at night as pulsing bands, curtains or streamers of reddish or greenish light, usually near the northern or southern magnetic pole. Auroras have also been observed on Saturn, Jupiter, Uranus and Neptune. Over three days in January 2004, ultraviolet detectors on the Cassini spacecraft recorded auroras on Saturn. These images were then superimposed on photos of Saturn taken by Hubble at the same time.

SATURN

The second largest planet, the least dense planet and the most beautiful planet, Saturn is a gigantic sphere that consists almost entirely of gas and clouds. It's so light, it could float in water— if an ocean big enough to hold it existed. More than nine times the Earth's diameter, Saturn is also nine times farther from the Sun than Earth, which means its rings and icy moons have been frozen rock-hard since the birth of the solar system 4.6 billion years ago.

January 24, 2004

January 26, 2004

January 28, 2004

THROWING SHADE
This close-up of Saturn shows the remarkable shadow cast on the planet by its rings. The image was taken by the Cassini spacecraft, which ended its 13-year study of Saturn in September 2017 in a scheduled "Grand Finale" maneuver. Following a series of close passes between Saturn and its rings, Cassini plunged into the planet's atmosphere and burned up like a meteor. This plan was designed to ensure that Saturn's moons remain pristine for future exploration.

➜ THE ICE PLANET Uranus, like Neptune, is an "ice giant" because it is made mostly of ices, such as water, ammonia and methane. Unlike all the other planets in the solar system, Uranus is tipped on its side, with its axis almost perpendicular to the Sun. In this composite image, using photos taken by Voyager 2 and Hubble, we see one of the planet's brighter rings (note that it is almost vertical) as well as the most spectacular auroras ever seen on Uranus. Auroras are created when streams of charged electrons from the Sun are caught in a planet's magnetic field and funneled into the upper atmosphere. There, they interact with gas particles and erupt in bursts of light. Hubble's ultraviolet images revealed that the auroras on Uranus actually rotate with the planet.

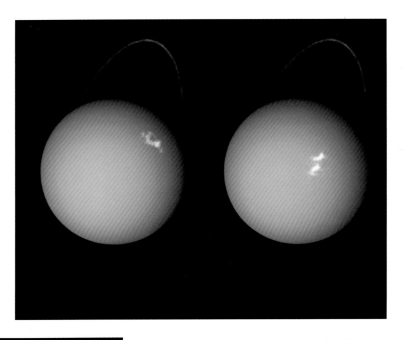

⬅ CLOUDS FROM ALL SIDES NOW

With one of the coldest atmospheres in the solar system, Neptune is the most distant planet from the Sun. It is 2.8 billion miles (4.5 billion km) away and takes roughly 165 years to make one orbit (the Earth's orbit is one year). To celebrate Neptune's first complete orbit since its discovery in 1846, Hubble used its Wide Field Camera 3 to take one photo every four hours on June 25/26, 2011, providing a full view of the planet's 16-hour daily rotation. The camera's ultraviolet to near-infrared wavelengths allow astronomers to study the structure of the planet's atmosphere. The pink clouds in its northern and southern hemispheres are made of methane ice crystals and reflect near-infrared light. The absorption of red light by Neptune's methane atmosphere gives the planet its aqua color. Like Uranus, Neptune's interior is made of ice and rock.

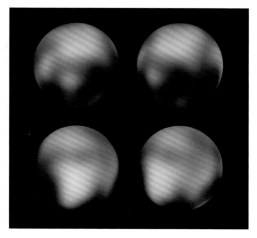

↑ **HUBBLE'S LIMITATIONS** Some objects remain beyond Hubble's reach. The dwarf planet Pluto is simply too small and too far away for Hubble to capture in detail. But before the New Horizons spacecraft flew past Pluto in 2015, the four Hubble images above were the best view we had of the distant planet. They were created using multiple Hubble images taken in 2002 and 2003, and it took 20 computers running continuously for four years to produce them.

↑ **A BETTER LOOK** After a six-year journey, NASA's New Horizons spacecraft reached the Kuiper belt and Pluto in 2015. It sent back remarkably detailed pictures of Pluto and its moon Charon. This composite shot shows the relative size of Charon and Pluto but is not an accurate representation of their distance from each other.

THE DEMOTION OF PLUTO Pluto is located in the outer solar system in the Kuiper belt—a much larger asteroid belt than the one that swirls around the inner solar system. Pluto's existence was confirmed in 1930, but its designation as a planet was debated almost from the start. Eventually, telescopes located an object in the Kuiper belt that is larger than Pluto, putting the ninth planet on life support. In 2006, the International Astronomical Union made it official: Pluto, named after the god of the underworld, was demoted to the status of a dwarf planet.

**CENTER OF THE
CAT'S EYE
NEBULA**

MIRROR IMAGE Here's a puzzle: How can you take a photograph of the exterior of your house while you're inside it? The answer is, you can't. For the same reason, we are unable to photograph the entire Milky Way Galaxy because Earth is located inside it.

But as luck would have it, 30 million light-years away from Earth, the Milky Way has a cosmic twin known as NGC6744. Like our home galaxy, this is a barred spiral galaxy. In this type of galaxy, the arms spiral out not from the center but from the ends of a straight bar of old yellow stars that runs across the middle of the galaxy. The spiral arms appear in shades of pink and blue. The pink regions are where stars have recently been born, and the blue areas contain young star clusters.

STAR CLUSTERS, NEBULAS AND THE MILKY WAY

When we look overhead on a clear, moonless evening in late summer, away from city lights, we see a sky full of stars. This is our cosmic neighborhood, a small corner of the Milky Way Galaxy in which we live.

In this chapter, Hubble turns its gaze to celestial bodies within the Milky Way Galaxy and just beyond. Many of these objects are identified by a number assigned to them three centuries ago by a French astronomer named Charles Messier. Searching for comets was his passion. In his quest, he often spotted fuzzy splotches of light that looked like comets. But on closer inspection, he found they were distant galaxies, star clusters or nebulas. To avoid this confusion, he compiled a list of 110 of these celestial objects.

The building blocks of every galaxy, stars are born in enormous clouds of gas and dust known as nebulas. In the regions where stars are forming, bright nebulas dot the galaxy's spiral arms, appearing pinkish in color photographs. These star nurseries give birth to clusters of stars, dense spherical swarms of hundreds of thousands of stars. The clusters eventually migrate throughout the spiral arms.

With dazzling portraits that record the births, lives and deaths of some of our brightest, youngest and oldest stars, Hubble helps us better understand the galaxy we call home.

SCUTUM-CENTAURUS ARM

SAGITTARIUS ARM

NORMA ARM

SAGITTARIUS ARM

PERSEUS ARM

OUTER ARM

ORION SPUR

PERSEUS ARM

STARRY, STARRY NIGHT Humans have gazed up at the night sky with wonder since there were humans on Earth. And on a clear, dark night away from city lights, it's impossible to miss the broad, hazy path that washes across the sky. The Greeks called it *galaxios kyklos* (milky circle), while the Romans named it *via lacea* (milky road). We call it the Milky Way. What we are looking at is a sector of the spiral galaxy where we live. It is filled with stars, gas and dust—all held together by gravity.

⬆ **X MARKS THE SUN** The Milky Way Galaxy is a barred spiral galaxy. It has a bar-shaped center of old yellow stars. Graceful arms of younger stars pinwheel out from the ends of the bar, illuminating the interstellar gas and dust. The names of the galaxy's arms are shown in this NASA illustration. Our solar system is found in a minor arm called the Orion Spur. The "x" marks the location of our Sun.

NORTHERN HEMISPHERE
SUMMER MILKY WAY

NORTHERN HEMISPHERE
WINTER MILKY WAY

SOUTHERN HEMISPHERE
MILKY WAY

⬆ WHAT'S UP As residents of the Milky Way Galaxy, we observe it from within, and which part of the galaxy we're seeing depends on where we are on Earth and the season. In the summer, from the northern hemisphere, we are gazing at the Sagittarius Arm of the Milky Way, straight through to the galaxy's core, where the population of stars is greater and therefore brighter. In the winter, we look out to the Perseus Arm and the outer regions of the galaxy.

⬅ WE CAN SEE CLEARLY NOW The European Southern Observatory's Very Large Telescope is located in the middle of the Atacama Desert, in Chile. This site was selected because it is the driest, clearest place on Earth for scanning the universe. Four massive telescopes are used every night for astronomical research and are often teamed up with the Hubble Space Telescope. In the image at left, the starry Milky Way shines overhead, far away from the glow of city lights or the fog of atmospheric dust and pollution. Only the Hubble has a better view. The bright blob visible just below center is the Large Magellanic Cloud, a satellite galaxy of the Milky Way.

MILKY WAY GALAXY

← **CRUSH AT THE CENTER** Peering across 27,000 light-years, Hubble's near-infrared vision penetrates lanes of interstellar dust to photograph the very center of our Milky Way Galaxy. Like the downtown of a bustling city, the core is very crowded. The bright blue stars in the image are foreground stars. The red stars are shrouded in dust. Dense clouds of gas and dust are outlined against the background stars. At the center of the galaxy is a supermassive black hole, a region of space with a gravitational field so intense that no matter can escape. A dense star cluster of 10 million stars surrounds the black hole.

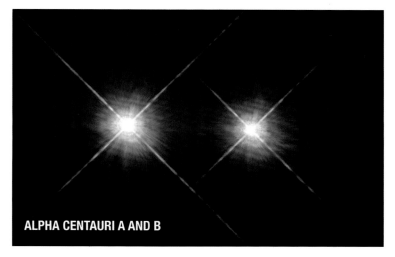

ALPHA CENTAURI A AND B

SIRIUS A (AND B)

↑ **BIG, BRIGHT AND BEAUTIFUL** Only 8.6 light-years from Earth, Sirius A is the brightest star in our nighttime sky. In this image, Sirius A is shown along with its companion Sirius B (the tiny dot at lower left), a white dwarf star. Because of its small size (just slightly larger than Earth), Sirius B is very faint. Overexposing the image of Sirius A has made the dim Sirius B visible. The two stars revolve around each other once every 50 years. The cross-shaped spikes and rings around Sirius A are produced within the Hubble Space Telescope's imaging system.

↑ **DOUBLE VISION** What looks like a pair of car headlights approaching us on a dark country road is actually a Hubble portrait of the closest star system to Earth, the Alpha Centauri group. Its members include Alpha Centauri A (left), Alpha Centauri B (right) and the faint red dwarf star Proxima Centauri, which is not in this image because it lies one trillion miles (1.6 trillion km) from the other two.

Alpha Centauri A is only slightly bigger than our Sun and has a similar temperature. Alpha Centauri B is a little smaller and cooler. Like a pair of skaters, the two stars pivot around each other, completing an orbit in 80 years. Proxima Centauri takes a whopping 500,000 years to make one orbit about its companion stars. Located 4.3 light-years from Earth, the Alpha Centauri group is roughly 270,000 times the distance from Earth to the Sun. An interstellar probe traveling at one-tenth the speed of light could reach the system in a little over 40 years.

NGC6752

PALOMAR 1

← THE ODDBALL Palomar 1 is a faint globular star cluster located in the constellation Cepheus, in one of the Milky Way's outer spiral arms. It is probably half the age of most globular star clusters, suggesting that Palomar 1 formed in a different way than other clusters. It may be the leftover core of a small galaxy that strayed too close to the Milky Way and was torn apart by gravitational forces. Over billions of years, our galaxy has a history of eating up such unlucky galaxies.

↓ GENERATION GAP Most of a cluster's stars are formed at the same time. As these stars age and cool, they become red giants. Their outer shell expands and burns in a reddish color as their center collapses. You can see many of these stars in the photo of the star cluster Messier 5 (M5) below. But star clusters can also be home to young blue stars, called blue stragglers. These stars may have been created when stars collided or when two stars sharing the same orbit merged to form one star. M5 is located in the constellation Serpens.

THE WONDER OF GLOBULAR STAR CLUSTERS

Globular star clusters can contain 10,000 to 1 billion stars that are so tightly bound by gravity, they form a spherical shape. The average distance between stars can be as little as one light-year. At the brightly lit center, the stars are densely packed. Globular star clusters orbit the core of galaxies like satellites. At least 150 globular clusters orbit the Milky Way Galaxy's flat spiral disk. Carrying the leftovers from the clusters that formed the Milky Way roughly 12 billion years ago, they hold our galaxy's oldest stars. Galaxies larger than the Milky Way can have thousands of globular star clusters.

M5

← GLITTERATI There's a whole lot of bling going on in the globular star cluster NGC6752, the third brightest cluster in the sky. At more than 11 billion years old, it is one of the oldest groupings of stars known. It has been blazing for well over twice as long as our solar system has existed. NGC6752 is about 13,000 light-years from Earth and is located in the southern constellation Pavo.

→ **OMEGA CENTAURI** The brightest and most massive globular cluster in the Milky Way, Omega Centauri is a huge nest of one billion stars. It contains aging red giants, brilliant blue stars, tiny white stars and the remains of burned-out stars.

OMEGA CENTAURI

M13

↑ **MESSIER 13** This Hubble portrait of the core of the globular cluster Messier 13 (M13) offers a clear view of the hundreds of thousands of stars in the central region. One of the best-known clusters in the northern sky, M13 is found in the constellation Hercules, 25,000 light-years away.

M15

↑ **MESSIER 15** One of the densest globular star clusters, Messier 15 (M15) contains stars that are about 13 billion years old — the oldest-known objects in the universe.

M9

↑ **MESSIER 9** Hubble's image of globular star cluster Messier 9 (M9) shows 250,000 stars swarming in a spherical clcud.

M71

← **MESSIER 71** Because of its loose arrangement of stars, Messier 71 (M71) does not resemble a typical globular star cluster. It is about 12 billion years old, roughly the same age as most globular clusters. M71 is 13,000 light-years from Earth and 27 light-years across.

OPEN STAR CLUSTERS

In addition to globular star clusters, there are open star clusters. An open star cluster is a group of young stars briefly held together by gravity. The clusters are born inside dense clouds of matter in our galaxy. Most open clusters have a short life, usually breaking apart in less than 100 million years. The member stars then continue to orbit our galaxy as individuals. More than 1,100 open star clusters have been discovered in the Milky Way Galaxy.

THE PLEIADES

↑ **THE PLEIADES** Also known as the Seven Sisters, this open star cluster contains several hundred stars, seven of which are visible to the naked eye from Earth. Only 400 light-years from Earth, the Pleiades cluster can be found in the winter sky near the shoulder of Taurus the bull.

→ **WESTERLUND 2** Located in the constellation Carina, Westerlund 2 contains some of our galaxy's hottest, brightest and most massive stars. This compact young star cluster is probably only one to two million years old. In this Hubble image, we see a brilliant tapestry of young stars flaring to life.

WESTERLUND 2

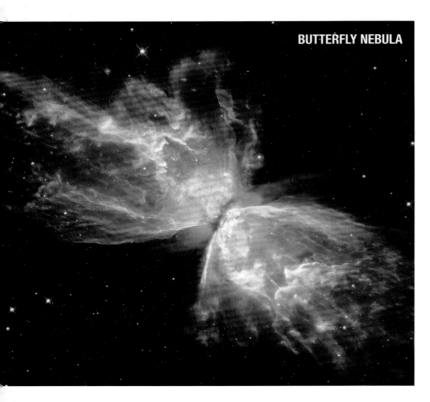

BUTTERFLY NEBULA

← **WINGING IT**   The delicate-looking Butterfly Nebula is anything but delicate. Its "wings" are formed by churning bubbles of gas heated to more than 36,000 degrees F (20,000°C). This gas roars into space at over 620,000 miles (one million km) per hour. Hidden inside a dark, doughnut-shaped ring of dust, the dying star at its center is about five times the mass of the Sun. This thick dust belt pinches the nebula in the middle, creating its hourglass shape. The glowing gas that forms the star's outer layer was expelled roughly 2,000 years ago. The Butterfly's "wingspan" measures more than two light-years.

↓ **ON THE MARCH**   The Ant Nebula, another member of Hubble's celestial zoo, looks like the head and thorax of a garden ant. Its central star might have a closely orbiting companion whose gravity is shaping the outflowing gas. This Hubble image reveals 100 times more detail than can be observed with telescopes on Earth. Discovered in 1922, the Ant Nebula is located in the southern constellation Norma.

↓ **WEB MASTER**   When powerful stellar winds blasted off the central star of the Red Spider Nebula, they created a wavelike pattern of ripples 62 billion miles (100 billion km) high. The central star is at least 540,000 degrees F (300,000°C), making it one of the hottest stars known. This nebula is located 3,000 light-years away, in the constellation Sagittarius.

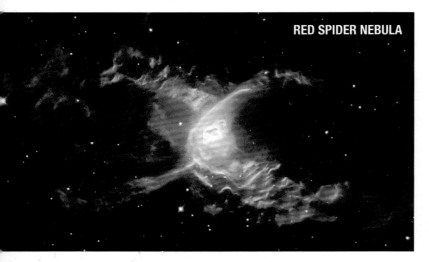

RED SPIDER NEBULA

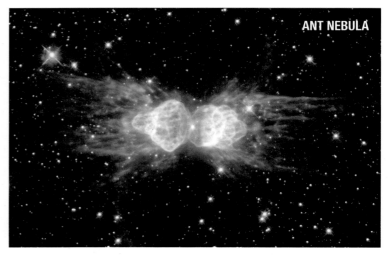

ANT NEBULA

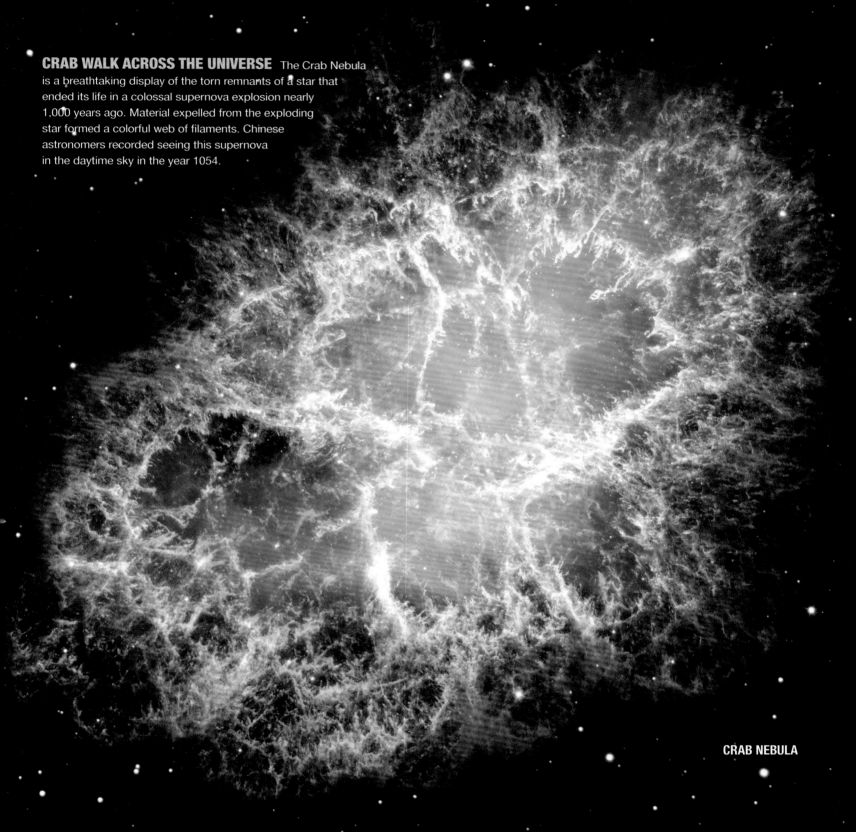

CRAB WALK ACROSS THE UNIVERSE The Crab Nebula is a breathtaking display of the torn remnants of a star that ended its life in a colossal supernova explosion nearly 1,000 years ago. Material expelled from the exploding star formed a colorful web of filaments. Chinese astronomers recorded seeing this supernova in the daytime sky in the year 1054.

CRAB NEBULA

SNOW ANGEL NEBULA

← HEAVENLY FLIGHT The aptly named Snow Angel Nebula, also known as S106, is a star-forming region located in the constellation Cygnus, nearly 2,000 light-years from Earth. A massive young star at the center of the nebula is responsible for all the activity we see. Twin lobes of superhot gas, glowing blue in this image, stretch outward from the central star to form the angel's wings. A ring of dust and gas orbiting the star acts like a belt, cinching the expanding nebula in the middle. Hubble's keen eye reveals ripples and ridges in the hot gas as it interacts with its cooler surroundings.

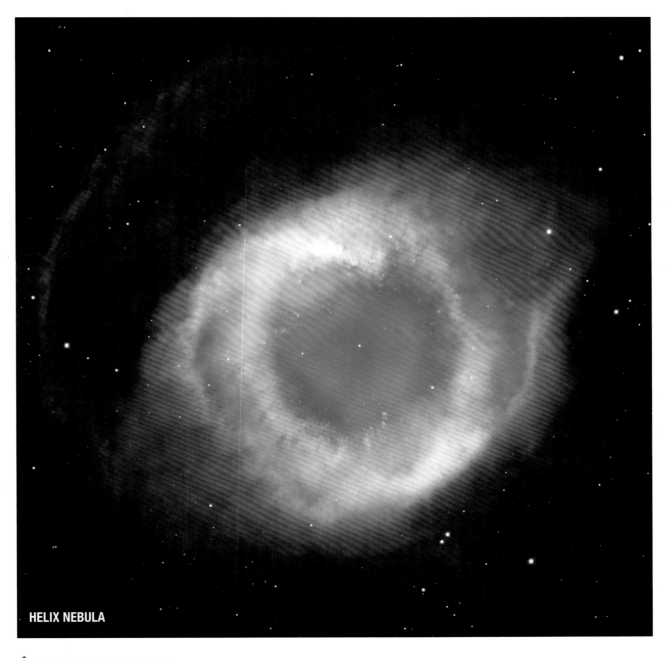

HELIX NEBULA

↑ SMALL BUT SIZZLING The Helix Nebula looks like a bubble because it is nearly face-on to Earth, but we are actually gazing into an open tunnel of glowing gases. Along the inner rim of the nebula, thousands of filaments point back toward the central star, which is a small, superhot white dwarf. These filaments formed when a hot wind of gas punched through colder dust and gas thrown off by the dying star.

BUBBLE NEBULA

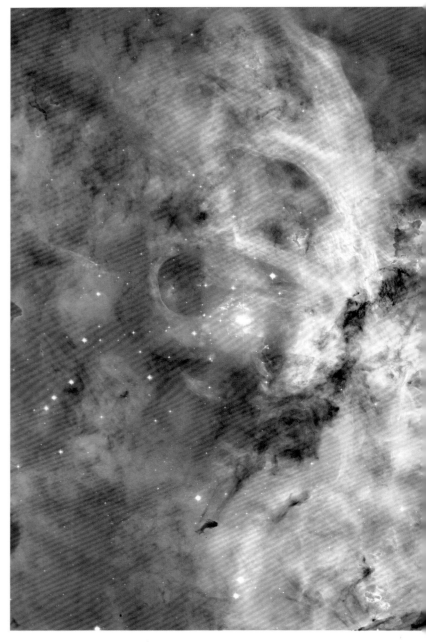

↑ BLOW UP Like a runaway balloon floating among the stars, the Bubble Nebula, also known as NGC7635, is inflating at the rate of 24,000 miles (38,600 km) per hour. How did this bubble form? An ultrahot young star several hundred thousand times brighter than our Sun and 45 times more massive is producing a fierce stellar wind and intense radiation. These have inflated a glowing bubble of gas that pushes against denser material. The Bubble Nebula lies 8,000 light-years away, in the constellation Cassiopeia.

CARINA NEBULA

↑ **MASSIVE AND MESSY** Three million years ago, stars began to form in the middle of a huge cloud of cold hydrogen gas in the Carina Nebula, the largest star-forming region in the Milky Way Galaxy. The area shown in this photo is 50 light-years across, only a small portion of the 460-light-year-wide nebula. This immense stellar nursery is 7,500 light-years distant.

45

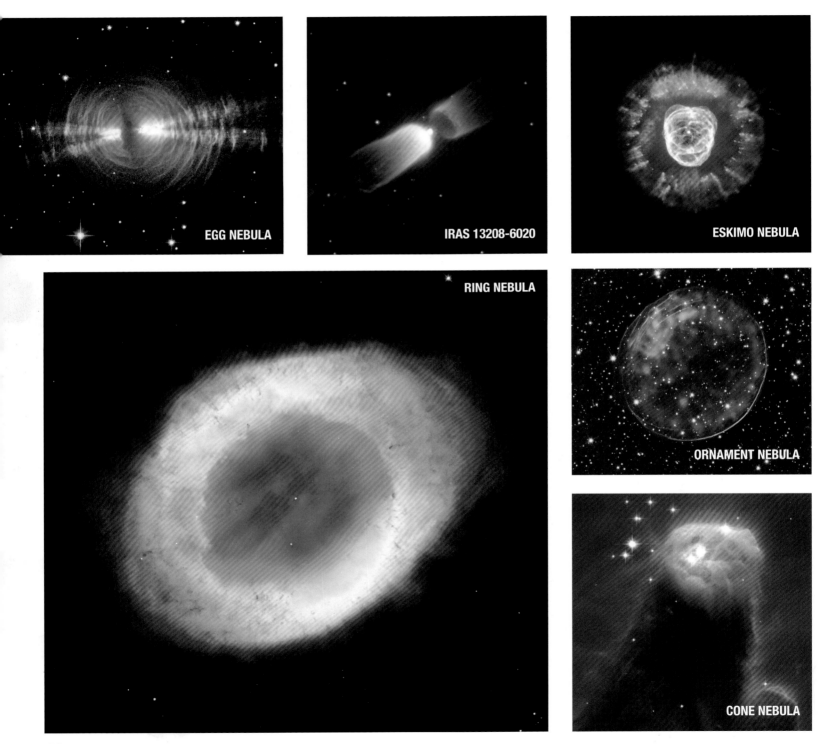

EGG NEBULA

IRAS 13208-6020

ESKIMO NEBULA

RING NEBULA

ORNAMENT NEBULA

CONE NEBULA

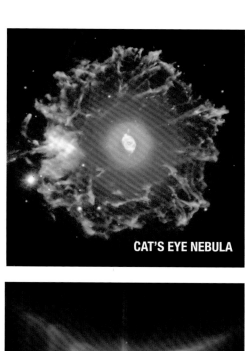

CAT'S EYE NEBULA

VEIL NEBULA

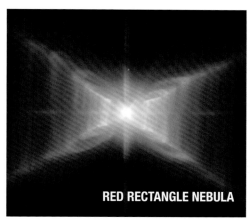

RED RECTANGLE NEBULA

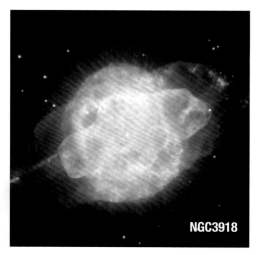

NGC3918

SPIROGRAPH NEBULA

NECKLACE NEBULA

HORSEHEAD NEBULA

Also known as Messier 42 (M42), the Orion Nebula resides in the constellation Orion, just below the belt of the mythological hunter. On a dark night, it is visible to the naked eye as a small, hazy cloud. Four dazzling stars, called the Trapezium, were born together at the heart of the nebula. Each of these stars is much hotter and more massive than our Sun, and their radiation causes the entire nebula to glow. This interstellar cave is ballooning under the pressure of starlight. The warm, pastel colors in the nebula are largely due to glowing hydrogen. In a Hubble photographic survey of the nebula, more than 3,000 stars have been detected. Thanks to Hubble's detailed images, NASA scientists consider this nebula "a laboratory for studying the star-formation process."

➜ **THE FULL PICTURE** Only 1,500 light-years away, the Orion Nebula is the closest large star-forming region to Earth. It is estimated to be 24 light-years across and is roughly 2,000 times the mass of our Sun. This stellar nursery has been known to many cultures throughout human history. The Maya of Mesoamerica believed the nebula was the cosmic fire of creation. They pretty much nailed it. The Orion Nebula is an enormous cloud of dust and gas where vast numbers of new stars are being born. Although the nebula looks flat in a photograph, we are actually looking into a cave-shaped cloud of glowing gases.

⬆ **THE HORSE UP CLOSE** One of the most familiar celestial objects, the Horsehead Nebula looks like a giant seahorse rising from storm-tossed waters. This towering pillar of hydrogen laced with cold dust has been imaged countless times, but Hubble shows us the horse in a different light by photographing it in infrared. This allows the camera to pierce through the dusty material that usually hides the nebula's interior. In the resulting photo, we see a fragile-looking structure made of delicate folds of gas. Astronomers estimate that the Horsehead will be destroyed by the blistering radiation from nearby hot massive stars in about five million years. The nebula lies 1,600 light-years away, in the constellation Orion.

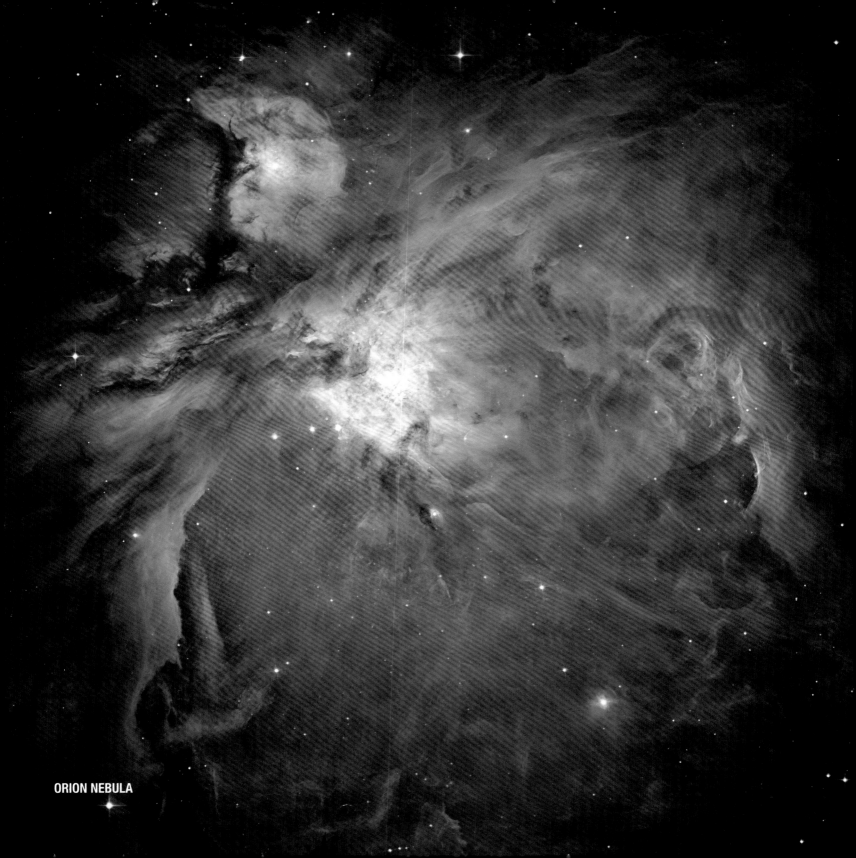

ORION NEBULA

EAGLE NEBULA

↑ LONG REACH This vast lane of dust and gas, part of the Eagle Nebula, is 9.5 light-years long, twice the distance from our Sun to Alpha Centauri, the nearest star. It looks like a gash in a gigantic, billowy cloud. Ghostly streamers of gas boiling off the surface create a haze around the structure, which is silhouetted against a background of more distant gas.

➜ PILLAR POWER The most famous celestial target ever photographed by Hubble is the Eagle Nebula (M16), the so-called Pillars of Creation. Hubble's Wide Field Camera 3 produced a mosaic image that stretches down to the base of the pillars. Three giant columns of cold gas are bathed in the scorching ultraviolet light from a cluster of young massive stars embedded in the nebula. The winds from these stars are slowly eroding the towers of gas and dust. Although such features are common in star-forming regions, the M16 pillars are, by far, the most haunting. The bluish haze around the dense edges of the pillars is material that is heating up and evaporating into space. The pillars are so far away, the light that Hubble recorded for this image left them 6,500 years ago.

EAGLE NEBULA

RS PUPPIS

CALABASH NEBULA

↑ JET PROPULSION At first glance, this bizarre-looking object might be some kind of interstellar starship. The Calabash Nebula is an example of a brief stage in the death of a star like our Sun. The aging star is rapidly changing from a bloated red giant to a planetary nebula. During this period, the outer layers of the star's atmosphere are so hot that they escape deep into space along the doomed star's axis. The jetlike exhaust is being propelled at 620,000 miles (one million km) per hour.

← TWINKLE TWINKLE Looking like a glittering holiday wreath, the bright star RS Puppis is cocooned in reflective dust illuminated by the star. RS Puppis burned steadily for most of its life, slowly consuming the hydrogen fuel at its core to keep it shining brightly. However, when most of the fuel was gone, the star became unstable. It now expands and shrinks over 40 days, growing brighter and dimmer. The nebula surrounding RS Puppis formed from the dust and gas puffed off into space by the dying star.

↓ COSMIC DUST-UP The intense radiation from a hot young star has sculpted a cold cloud of hydrogen and dust into a fantasy landscape on the edge of NGC2174. Young white stars dot the glowing clouds, pushing away the dark star nurseries where they were born. Brown and rust-colored dust clouds that are producing new stars billow outward against a background of bright blue gas. These clouds will likely be dispersed by the energetic young star within a few million years. This star-forming region is 6,400 light-years away, in the constellation Orion.

NGC2174

**SPIRAL GALAXY
NGC5584**

BEYOND THE MILKY WAY

A galaxy is a stellar city containing vast numbers of stars, nebulas, planets and comets as well as huge quantities of gas and dust. Trillions of stars reside in the largest galaxies, while the smaller galaxies may have only a few hundred thousand stars. Galaxies may be found on their own or in clusters.

Like snowflakes, every galaxy is distinct. There are three basic types of galaxies. A *spiral galaxy* has long, stellar arms winding around a large central bulge, like a celestial pinwheel. Our Milky Way is a spiral galaxy. An *elliptical galaxy* can be shaped like a sphere or a football and is made up of immense swarms of stars. An *irregular galaxy* is a loose collection of stars with no distinct structure.

Astronomers estimate that the known universe contains at least 100 billion galaxies. Three are close enough to us that we can spot them in a clear, dark sky. The Andromeda Galaxy, roughly 2.5 million light-years away, is visible from the northern hemisphere, and the Large and Small Magellanic Clouds, about 160,000 light-years away, can be viewed from the southern hemisphere. They're all part of what astronomers call the Local Group, which includes the Milky Way.

Like no other telescope before it, the Hubble Space Telescope sees remote galaxies with remarkable clarity and sharpness. In this chapter, we feature Hubble's impressive images of galaxies that neighbor the Milky Way.

LARGE MAGELLANIC CLOUD

LARGE MAGELLANIC CLOUD

⬇ **STAR-MAKING MACHINE** Embedded in the Tarantula Nebula, in the Large Magellanic Cloud, 30 Doradus has been creating new stars at a furious pace for millions of years. This Hubble image depicting a portion of 30 Doradus is a segment of the largest digital mosaic ever created. In the full mosaic, Hubble revealed the stages of a star's life, from infant stars only a few thousand years old to monsters that die young in supernova explosions. The star clusters shown here range in age from roughly 2 million to 25 million years old.

30 DORADUS

⬆ **FROM A DISTANCE** An irregular galaxy, the Large Magellanic Cloud is one of many treasures of the southern night sky that is not visible to observers in the northern hemisphere. Although only $\frac{1}{50}$ the mass of the Milky Way, the Large Magellanic Cloud contains the biggest and most active star-forming nebula known in our part of the universe: the mighty Tarantula Nebula. It churns out stars at 10 times the rate of the Milky Way Galaxy.

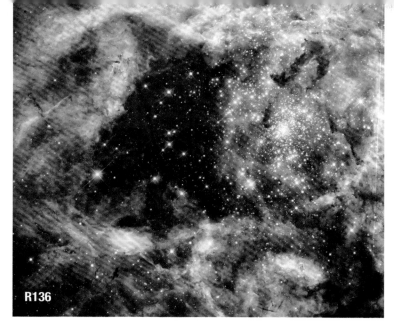

R136

← **BABIES ON BOARD** Known as R136, this massive stellar grouping is a turbulent region of star birth in the Tarantula Nebula, in the Large Magellanic Cloud. This Hubble image is the most detailed portrait yet of the largest star nursery in our local galactic neighborhood.

↓ **STARS AND CLOUDS** NGC1850, the second brightest star cluster in the Large Magellanic Cloud, is a type of object unknown in the Milky Way Galaxy. This young, globular-like star cluster has two parts: the large main cluster and a smaller cluster below and to the right. The large cluster is about 50 million years old, while its companion is only four million years old. Wisps of gas created by the explosion of short-lived, very massive stars surround NGC1850.

NGC1850

HUBBLE TAKES A CLOSER LOOK The image above is an up-close look at a slice of the Andromeda Galaxy, our neighbor in space. The portion of the galaxy shown is marked by the rectangular outline in the photo at left. The fine-grained structure of the spiral arms represents millions upon millions of individual stars in the big galaxy. The brighter stars are much closer to us. Some of them are just a few thousand light-years away in our home galaxy, the Milky Way.

When astronomers decided to use Hubble to obtain this very detailed portrait, they faced a mighty task. They had to "stitch" together 400 Hubble photos to complete the celestial jigsaw. The saw-toothed edges beyond the rectangular outline at left show the many individual frames that were required. This is the largest and sharpest view ever taken of the Andromeda Galaxy.

← WHOA!
Using Hubble, scientists tracked the motions of stars in the Andromeda Galaxy (at left in this illustration) and have concluded that it will eventually merge with the Milky Way Galaxy (the hazy band of light). Here, we see what the Earth's night sky might look like in four billion years.

OUR CLOSEST NEIGHBOR GALAXY
The Andromeda Galaxy is a spiral galaxy containing an enormous swarm of suns so remote that it takes more than two million years for its light to reach us. At 2.5 million light-years distant, the combined light of its 800 billion stars produces an image that is barely detectable to the unaided eye. Although the Andromeda Galaxy was once thought to be two to three times the size of our Milky Way Galaxy, recent research has found that the two galaxies are about the same size. Andromeda is the nearest major galaxy to the Milky Way.

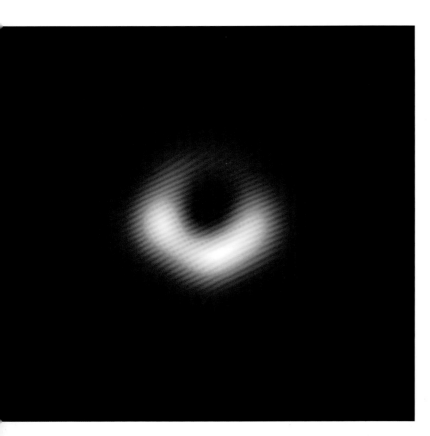

↑ HISTORIC SHOT In April 2019, an international team of researchers made headlines around the world by obtaining the first visual evidence of a black hole. To capture this elusive target at the center of the galaxy M87, a global network of eight radio telescopes was linked to form an Earth-sized virtual telescope known as the Event Horizon Telescope. M87 is located 55 million light-years from Earth, and the black hole at its core is 6.5 billion times more massive than our Sun. A fiery ring of light and gas marks the black hole's event horizon, the point of no return. There, light gets bent and twisted around as it is relentlessly sucked into the black abyss along with superheated gas and dust, never to be seen again. This remarkable image begins a new chapter in the study of black holes.

→ SMALL BUT POWERFUL At a distance of 15 million light-years, the Southern Pinwheel Galaxy, or Messier 83, is one of the closest barred spirals to Earth. It's so close that we can see it with binoculars. The Southern Pinwheel offers a colorful bird's-eye view of the architecture of a barred spiral galaxy. The spiral arms are etched by dark dust lanes, which stand out against a carpet of several thousand brilliant blue star clusters. Ultraviolet light produced by these clusters causes the surrounding gas clouds to glow reddish pink, like jewels in a cosmic necklace. This galaxy is less than half the size of the Milky Way.

SPIRAL GALAXIES

A spiral galaxy is a slowly rotating, pinwheel-shaped disk of stars, gas and dust with arms that sweep outward. The bright central bulge contains older, dimmer stars. New stars form mostly in the spiral arms. At the very center of a spiral galaxy is a supermassive black hole, a region with such intense gravity that nothing, even light, can escape it. There are two types of spiral galaxies. In a normal spiral, the arms coil out from the center. In a barred spiral, there is a bright bar of stars at the center, and the arms unwind from the ends of the bar. The Milky Way is a barred spiral galaxy.

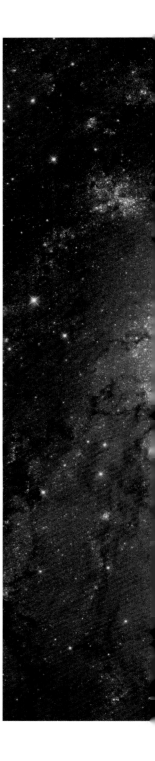

SOUTHERN PINWHEEL GALAXY

NGC2683

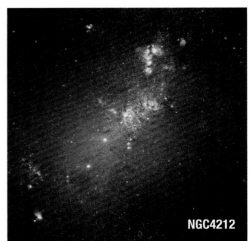

NGC4212

NGC2683 In this side view of spiral galaxy NGC2683, above, the dusty lanes of its spiral arms are shown against the golden haze of the galaxy's core.

NGC4212 It may be small, but dwarf galaxy NGC4212, above right, is packed with stars at every stage of their lives, from hot young suns to old clusters with red supergiant stars. This makes it an ideal laboratory to study how a star evolves.

NGC4696 Thread-like filaments of dust encircle the center of NGC4696, right, a giant elliptical galaxy. As they spiral inward, the filaments are consumed by a massive black hole at the galaxy's core.

THE MICE Nicknamed The Mice because of their long, streaming tails of stars and gas, these two colliding galaxies, below left, will eventually become a single giant elliptical galaxy. Material can be seen flowing between the galaxies.

SOMBRERO GALAXY Thick dust lanes containing newborn stars encircle a vast, glowing globe of light created by billions of old stars in the brilliant central bulge of the Sombrero Galaxy, below right. As seen from Earth, this galaxy is tilted nearly edge-on. It is located 28 million light-years away.

NGC4696

THE MICE

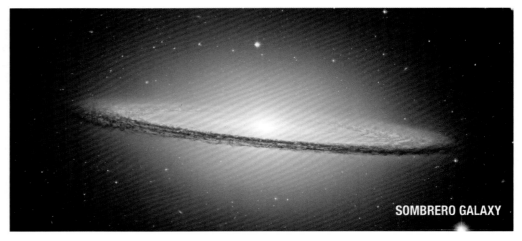

SOMBRERO GALAXY

WHIRLPOOL GALAXY

TADPOLE GALAXY

WHIRLPOOL GALAXY Bright pink star-forming regions trace the sweeping arms of the Whirlpool Galaxy, above left. A dwarf galaxy near the tip of one arm is passing behind the Whirlpool.

TADPOLE GALAXY Racing through space like a runaway pinwheel firework, the Tadpole Galaxy, above right, leaves behind a long tail of debris that stretches more than 280,000 light-years.

RING GALAXY This lovely blue tiara of stars, left, formed when two galaxies collided. As stars and gas were pushed outward by the resulting shock wave, gas clouds contracted to form new stars.

NGC4258 This spiral galaxy, below left, is thought to have a supermassive black hole at its center.

CARTWHEEL GALAXY The Cartwheel, below center, is the aftermath of a head-on collision with a smaller galaxy. New stars form the outer rim of the "wheel," and wisps of material are the spokes.

M82 What looks like flowing lava in spiral galaxy M82, below right, is hydrogen propelled outward by an explosion of star birth. This may have been triggered by a close brush with neighboring M81.

RING GALAXY

NGC4258

CARTWHEEL GALAXY

M82

NGC1300

⬆ **BARRED ENTRY** This stunning Hubble image of NGC1300 is a beautiful example of a barred spiral galaxy. In a typical spiral galaxy, the starry arms twist out from the center of the galaxy. In a barred spiral galaxy, a concentration of mostly older stars forms a bar that runs across the middle of the galaxy, and the arms curl outward from the ends of this bar. The arms contain blue clusters of young stars, glowing pink clouds where new stars are forming and dark lanes of dust.

➡ **HEY, NEIGHBOR!** In this view of the inner region of Messier 106 (M106), black dust clouds stand out against the bright glow of stars at the galaxy's core, which looks like a churning witch's cauldron. Two brilliant blue spiral arms of hot young stars wrap around this cauldron. But what sets this galaxy apart from other spirals is that it sports an extra pair of arms, seen here as ghostly red wisps swirling around its center. Astronomers think these arms may be related to a monster black hole that is gobbling up matter at the galaxy's center. Located a little over 20 million light-years away, Messier 106 is one of the nearest spiral galaxies to us.

M106

NGC1132

← SMOOTH SAILING Looking like a transparent celestial egg, NGC1132 was likely born from an enormous galactic pileup, when several galaxies collided and created the brilliant but fuzzy giant elliptical galaxy. Thousands of ancient globular clusters swarm around NGC1132, like bees around a hive. These are likely the survivors of the cataclysmic event. Numerous more distant galaxies are scattered across the blackness of space.

↓ FOUR'S COMPANY Stephan's Quintet is a breathtaking example of galaxies caught up in a gravitational tug-of-war that is distorting and reshaping them. The interactions among the reddish-colored galaxies have sparked a frenzy of star birth both inside and outside the galaxies. A pair of galaxies just above center in this image seem to be locked in a death grip. The galaxy at lower left is a mere spectator of the chaos unfolding in the background. It is 40 million light-years from Earth, while the remaining members of the quintet reside 290 million light-years away.

THE LOW-KEY ELLIPTICALS

The universe is a violent place, and collisions between galaxies are frequent. When spiral galaxies collide, they lose their pinwheel shape and morph into an elliptical galaxy. Unlike the dramatic and colorful spiral galaxies, elliptical galaxies are smooth and featureless. They range in shape from nearly spherical to very elongated and have no spiral arms. Ellipticals are usually found in compact groups of galaxies, where there is a lot of interaction among the galaxies. Constant mergers and collisions followed by periods of star formation increase the size of an elliptical galaxy and use up much of the gas needed to create new stars. As a result, ellipticals contain mostly old red stars and have a very low rate of star formation. With a cargo of hundreds of millions to trillions of stars, ellipticals are the biggest galaxies in the universe.

STEPHAN'S QUINTET

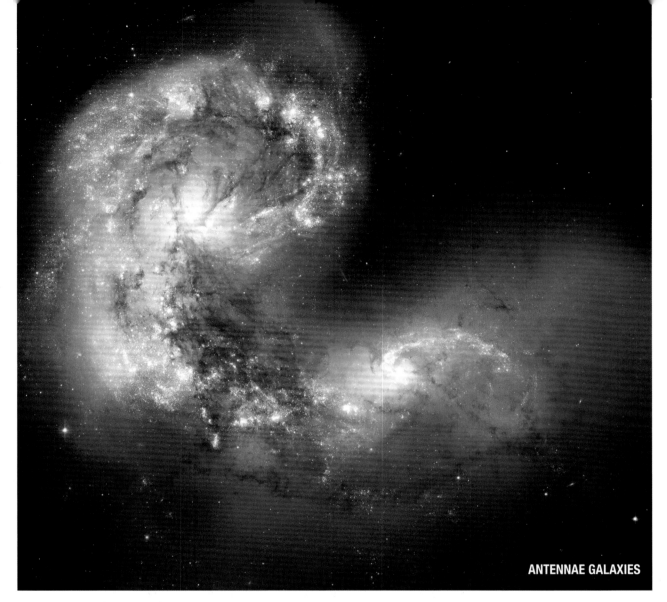

ANTENNAE GALAXIES

ANTENNAE

ANTENNAS UP Over a few hundred million years, two spiral galaxies were on a collision course that would end in a violent smashup and create the Antennae Galaxies. Stars that have been ripped from their parent galaxy form a brilliant arc between the wreckage of the two galaxies. Gas and dust thrown into space during the initial impact form two long sweeping tails that look like antennas in the image at left, which was taken from an observatory on Earth. Clusters of young stars sparkle in blue, while pinkish star-forming regions are cranking out even more stars. Astronomers estimate that this clash of galaxies will produce billions of new stars. The two orange blobs to the left and right of center are the cores of the ill-fated galaxies. Eventually, these cores will merge, and one large elliptical galaxy will remain.

GALAXY ROUNDUP Nearly every object in this photo is a galaxy containing billions of stars. The Coma cluster, a megalopolis of more than 1,000 galaxies, is so immense that it takes 20 million years for light to travel from one side of the cluster to the other. Most of the galaxies in the central portion of the cluster are ellipticals—enormous, featureless swarms of old stars. NGC4860, the brilliant glowing galaxy at the center of this image, is an elliptical. Young spiral galaxies reside in the outer regions of the cluster. We see one such spiral, NGC4858, to the left of its bright neighbor in this Hubble image. Its graceful spiral arms are dotted with fiery knots of material that seem to extend from the central part of the galaxy and tear away. Stars are being born here at such a high rate, scientists predict that NGC4858 will use up its gas long before it reaches the end of its life. Scattered in the spaces between the galaxies are the cluster's smallest members: globular star clusters. These globe-shaped clumps of stars contain several hundred thousand ancient suns. At a distance of 300 million light-years, the globular star clusters are mere points of light, even to Hubble's sharp eye.

PEERING INTO DARKNESS AND THE PAST

DISTANT GALAXIES

With the launch of the Hubble Space Telescope, we entered a new age of exploration. Like the intrepid early explorers navigating previously uncharted regions on Earth and forever changing our perspective of the world, Hubble has shown us places in the universe that no human before us has ever seen.

The universe was born in a black void 13.8 billion years ago from a cataclysmic explosion. Ever since then, the universe has been expanding outward from that one point of creation. The farther we look into space, the older the objects we see. Gazing deep into the cosmos, Hubble has captured portraits of the universe in its youth, when its densely packed matter was being jostled about like pinballs in an arcade game. It was a turbulent, chaotic time.

If we could look down on a miniature universe, everything we could see and scoop up with our hands—galaxies, nebulas, gas, stars, planets and dust—would add up to only 5 percent of the universe. The remaining 95 percent is dark matter and dark energy, which are invisible. Astronomers have determined they exist by the effect they have on matter in the visible universe. Just as we can't see gravity on Earth, we know it exists because we see the effect it has on objects. Throw a ball into the air, and it comes back down. Dark matter and dark energy are one of the greatest mysteries of the cosmos.

With its penetrating probe of deep space, the Hubble Space Telescope has been an invaluable partner in our quest to understand the origin and ultimate destiny of the universe.

D100

TOO CLOSE FOR COMFORT What looks like a flaming cosmic arrow that has scored a bull's-eye is a stream of dust and gas being stripped from a spiral galaxy called D100. Having strayed too close to the Coma galaxy cluster, D100 is being dragged into the center of the giant cluster by its intense gravitational pull. As it plunges inward, it plows through intergalactic matter, which pushes dust and gas from the galaxy into a tail that stretches 200,000 light-years into space. This image combines a Hubble view of the doomed spiral galaxy with a photo of the red tail of hydrogen gas taken by the Subaru Telescope, in Hawaii. In the Hubble image at right, the dark brown streaks near D100's central region are streamers of dust escaping from the galaxy. The bright blue glow in the tail is a clump of at least 200,000 young stars. In a few hundred million years, D100 will lose its spiral structure, its store of hydrogen fuel will be depleted and it will cease to produce new stars. It will become a dead galaxy containing only old stars.

D100

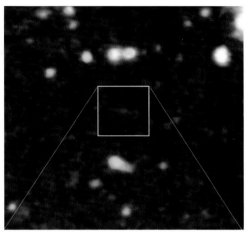

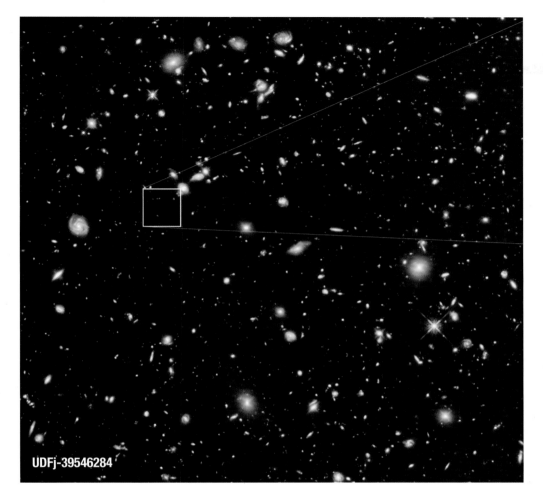

UDFj-39546284

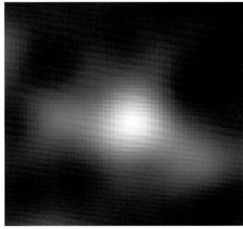

BLAST FROM THE PAST On the scale of the universe, distance is a time machine. The more distant something is, the longer its light takes to reach us and the younger it appears. Pushing the Hubble Space Telescope to its limits in 2011, astronomers found what they thought might be the most distant and ancient galaxy ever seen: UDFj-39546284. However, further imaging has thrown that into doubt. It appears as a faint dot of starlight (outlined above) in this Hubble image. It is a tiny, compact galaxy of blue stars (magnified at top and bottom right) that is too small and too young to have developed the familiar spiral shape. It would take more than 100 mini galaxies like this to make a galaxy the size of our Milky Way.

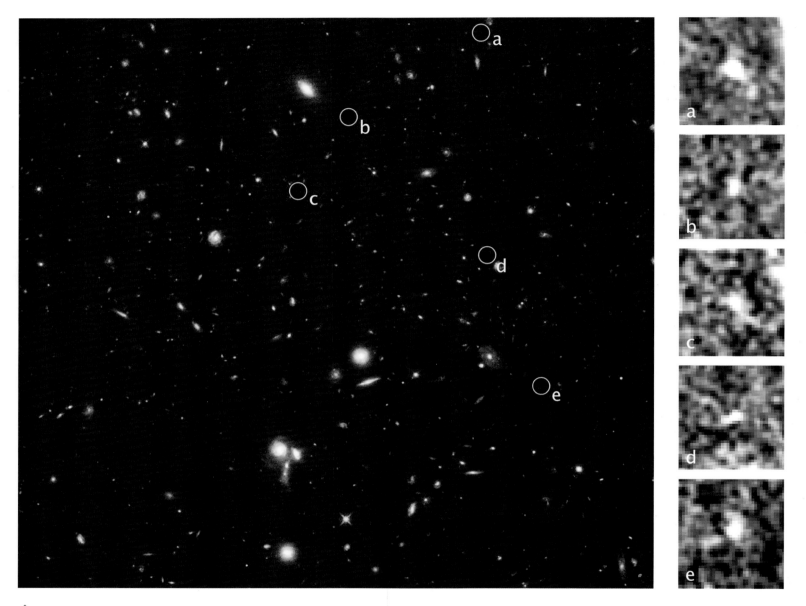

↑ **EARLIEST GALAXIES** Hubble has discovered a developing cluster of five young galaxies (circled and lettered above) 13.1 billion light-years away. The inset photos give us a closer look. The tiny galaxies were forming when the universe was just 600 million years old. Although they are only a fraction the size of the Milky Way, they are comparable in brightness because they are being fueled by large amounts of gas through mergers with other galaxies.

→ **BIG EYE IN THE SKY** Like a dazzling display of fireflies on a dark summer's night, galaxies zip around a galaxy cluster called Abell S1063, colliding and merging to build massive elliptical galaxies. With a staggering population of 1,000 galaxies, Abell S1063 has the mass of 100 trillion Suns. This huge mass acts like a cosmic magnifying glass, allowing us to see more distant galaxies that would otherwise be too faint to observe. The wispy bluish arcs are magnified galaxies that are about twice as far away.

ABELL S1063

GALAXIES FAR, FAR AWAY With its unblinking eye, the Hubble Space Telescope captured our deepest ever view of the universe, which is shown on these two pages and the following two pages. To obtain this image required a time exposure of more than 270 hours. It covers a patch of sky the size of the tip of a needle and contains a remarkable 10,000 galaxies. Ready to start counting?

INDEX

PHOTO CREDITS